Wilfred Campbell

The Dread Voyage

Poems

Wilfred Campbell

The Dread Voyage
Poems

ISBN/EAN: 9783744714037

Printed in Europe, USA, Canada, Australia, Japan

Cover: Foto ©Thomas Meinert / pixelio.de

More available books at **www.hansebooks.com**

THE DREAD VOYAGE

POEMS

BY

WILLIAM WILFRED CAMPBELL.

AUTHOR OF "LAKE LYRICS".

Toronto

WILLIAM BRIGGS

MONTREAL: C. W. COATES HALIFAX: S. F. HUESTIS

1893

TO

ALEXANDER McNEILL, Esq.,

AND

R. C. WELDON, Ph.D.,

THIS VOLUME IS AFFECTIONATELY

DEDICATED.

Ottawa, March, 1893.

CONTENTS.

THE DREAD VOYAGE.

TRIM the sails the weird stars under—
Past the iron hail and thunder,
Past the mystery and the wonder,
　　Sails our fated bark;
Past the myriad voices hailing,
Past the moaning and the wailing,
The far voices failing, failing,
　　Drive we to the dark.

Past the headlands grim and sombre,
Past the shores of mist and slumber,
Leagues on leagues no man may number,
　　Soundings none can mark;

While the olden voices calling,
One by one behind are falling;
Into silence dread, appalling,
Drift we to the dark.

Far behind, the sad eyes yearning,
Hands that wring for our returning,
Lamps of love yet vainly burning:
Past the headlands stark!
Through the wintry snows and sleeting,
On our pallid faces beating,
Through the phantom twilight fleeting.
Drive we to the dark.

Without knowledge, without warning,
Drive we to no lands of morning;
Far ahead no signals horning
Hail our nightward bark.

Hopeless, helpless, weird, outdriven,
Fateless, friendless, dread, unshriven,
For some race-doom unforgiven,
    Drive we to the dark.

Not one craven or unseemly;
In the flare-light gleaming dimly,
Each ghost-face is watching grimly:
    Past the headlands stark!
Hearts wherein no hope may waken,
Like the clouds of night wind-shaken,
Chartless, anchorless, forsaken,
    Drift we to the dark.

WINTER.

OVER these wastes, these endless wastes of white,
Rounding about far, lonely regions of sky,
Winter the wild-tongued cometh with clamorous might;
Deep-sounding and surgent, his armies of storm sweep by,
Wracking the skeleton woods and opens that lie
Far to the seaward reaches that thunder and moan,
Where barrens and mists and beaches forever are lone.

Morning shrinks closer to night, and nebulous noon
Hangs, a dull lanthorn, over the windings of snows;
And like a pale beech-leaf fluttering upward, the moon
Out of the short day, wakens and blossoms and grows,
And builds her wan beauty like to the ghost of a rose

Over the soundless silences, shrunken, that dream
Their prisoned deathliness under the gold of her beam.

Wide is the arch of the night, blue spangled with fire,
From wizened edge to edge of the shrivelled-up earth,
Where the chords of the dark are as tense as the strings of a lyre
Strung by the fingers of silence ere sound had birth,
With far-off, alien echoes of morning and mirth,
That reach the tuned ear of the spirit, beaten upon
By the soundless tides of the wonder and glory of dawn.

The stars have faded and blurred in the spaces of night,
And over the snow-fringed edges wakens the morn,
Pallid and heatless, lifting its lustreless light
Over the skeleton woodlands and stretches forlorn,
Touching with pallor the forests, storm-haggard and torn;
Till out of the earth's edge the winter-god rises acold,
And strikes on the iron of the month with finger of gold.

Then down the whole harp of the morning a vibration
rings,
Thrilling the heart of the dull earth with throbbings and
dreams
Of far-blown odours and music of long-vanished Springs ;
Till the lean, stalled cattle low for the lapping of streams,
And the clamorous cock, to the south, where his dung-
hill steams,
Looks the sun in the eye, and prophesies, hopeful and
clear,
The stir in the breast of the wrinkled, bleak rime of the
year.

THE LAST RIDE.

It seems his soul had lived that moment before, when he should come to the dread place.

I KNEW of it ages before,
Yea, it seemed that the years knew it too ;
That I should come to that shore,
Where the foam and the wild waters flew—
Where the winds and the bleak night blew ;—
And the name of that place, No More.

That he and she and death should ride together.

I knew of it ages ago,
That I should thunder that ride,
With her and the night for my woe—
With her and death by my side—
Her and her pitiful pride ;—
And the long hours whose shudd'ring flow

Where the black was as Eblis, and the sounds as worms moving in a grave.

Grew, while the black grew thick
As the close, hot air of a cave
In Eblis, where death-watches tick,
Like the moving of worms in a grave ;—
Grew, till the dawn outdrave
The black night, shudd'ring and sick.

The mimes chant their despair to the night.

Who were the mimes in the air
That wept for the woe of our flight,
That chanted a bitter despair,
To the dark, haunted heart of the night—
That knew not of wrong or of right,
Save but of the moments that were?

He sees the past, as ruined sunsets, and the early morning of life.

The ruins of sunsets that hung
On the far, reeling edge of the world ;—
The long-uttered thoughts that upsprung
Like the ghosts of a past that was furled,

Where the dreams of a life were impearled,
In a morning forevermore young!

She also knew the demons that haunted.

And she; she knew even as I,
Of the phantoms that haunted us there;
Of the demons that never could die,
While the world's heart pulsed our despair;
And out where the mad waters fare,
The ghostly, wan shorelands should lie.

They ride by the hoarse sea, and the bitter winds and hell with them.

O, that night, and that terrible ride—
With the bitter, sharp wind in the face,
And the hoarse, great tongues of the tide,
As it beat on the black of that place;
Till all hell joined in the race,
With death and despair for a guide!

He slays the foes of his guilty thoughts,

Many the foes that I slew,
With the sword of my guilt, red as blood—

while the demons trouble him.

Many the demons that blew
Their mad, flame-horns through my mood,
As I thundered that horrible wood,
To the place where a world went through.

Now he hates the morrows to come

White, meagre, the days yet to come
Seemed wintry and hateful to me:
Would mornings wake, pitiless, dumb,
With horror and dread agony—
And the moan of that terrible sea
Beat the dead-march of life like a drum,

with the remorse for his wrecked days.

In the hands of some hideous mime—
Some strange, inextinguishable flame
That would burn at my heart for all time—
Some horror too dread to have name,
As of one who had played for a game,
Then slipped and was lost in the slime?

He knows the end cometh.

(I am but the poor wreck of a man,)
When I came to that horrible place,
(Love was never a part of God's plan,)
And looked her and death in the face,
And knew me unworthy and base,
And the shores where the black waters ran;—

They come to the outer shore and look each on each through the mists, and read the ancient curse there,

When we came to that lone, outer shore,
Where the world sundered, parting us two;
(God and the dread nevermore!)
When we came where the thick mists blew,
So face could scarce on face, through,
Read the woe-rune of earth's ancient lore;—

and feel the dread agony of parting. Their souls feel for one another as the seas for the land.

When hand stretched longing for hand,
And that strange, wild cry of the soul;
As the feeble sea feels for the land,
Or a racer far, far from the goal;—

So we, ere we drank of death's dole,
Knew the black night that hope never
spanned.

But he knows the hour has come,

Then I knew as I looked on her face,
(Black, black is the night and the rain,)
Sweet as a flower in that place,
And heard the hoarse roar of the main;
That this was the hour for us twain,
The last, bitter end of the race.

and the anguish at the gate of the nevermore.

And I gripped her as man only grips
The last gift that God has for him,
And lived with my lips on her lips
An age that was anguished and dim;
And time was as bubbles that swim,
Or the hailing of out-faring ships.

They plead in vain with time while their

We pleaded and haggled with time,
With time who was haggard and hoar;

doom waits.

And met the dread hell of our crime,
While fate stood there at the door ;—
With our doom in his hand he upbore,
Till I heard each second's beat chime.

He feels that they died there. He is but a lost wreck on the coast of the ages ere the evil had power.

And I know now we died in that hour :—
I am all but the ghost of a man,
A mariner stranded ashore
On some continent out of God's plan,
Made before misery began,
Or evil got men in its power.

And dreams a dead life with but one thing real for him which he liveth over and over forever, that night and the woe that her face held.

In dreams my imaginings trace,
I feel I lived somewhere before,
Ere life was, in some phantom place,
Some land of the haunted No More ;—
But, O God, that night and that shore,
And that ride, and the woe of her face !

THE CONFESSION OF TAMA THE WISE.

WHEN all his days were ended and the time
Had come when he should ease his troubled breath,
And leave this world and all its joy and woe;
Tama the wise lay pondering on his bed,
Thinking of the silences to be;
And weary of the burden of his age
He breathed him hard and fained to. be at rest.

Then came there to him Augur the patriarch,
Who held the office of the national priest,
And kept the holy temple lamps alit,
And made himself a power athwart the land,

In good repute with people and with king,.
And spake to Tama :—
"Now that thou art passing
Out to the place of peace the gods have given,
To those who did them honour here on earth,
And have lived justly with their fellowmen,
'Tis meet that I who am their herald here,
Should read to thee from out the holy scrolls,
And hear from thee wherein thy heart hath sinned,
And make with thee libation to the Name.
And give thee hope that now thy toil is done,
Thou wilt go hence to dwell with the high gods,
Not with the flaming ones who sink in Hell,
But, recreate, in gardens of the light."

Then spake old Tama :—
"Shame not the Eternal
With mouth of empty words of what thou knowest
No more than do the hollow winds that blow

From the four corners of the vacuous heaven;
Nor think to bribe the darkness with thy gifts,
Nor fill with fancied flame the senseless void;
For that old law that rules all from the first
Hath given each thing its place: and what is life,
But the quick flame that leaps up from the hearth,
Until the brand it feeds on is consumed?
And what art thou, O Augur, what am I,
That thou shouldst play the god and I the fool,
And dream that thou canst hold the keys of being,
And in some fabled existence yet to be,
Canst lease me joy or sorrow at thy will?

"O Augur, knowest thou not me, Tama of old time,
That I am not the man to act the dupe;
Or dost thou think that lying on my bed
In mine old age, like some slow-crumbling tree,
That I may chance grow credulous like a child
Or woman or weakling, and at fear of death

In my dark hour of dissolution's throe,
Accept a dream I never knew in life,
And mock the Eternal, man and mine own self,
With some weird vision born of fear and doubt,
But never dreamed of wisdom or of strength?

"O Augur, from the cradle to the tomb,
All things about us teach us we must pass.
The joys we knew as children, the long years,
That slowly closed about us like a prison,
The summer grasses underneath our feet,
The winter snows, the joyous spring-tide hours,
All spake the awful future in my heart,
And whispered, all is passing, thou must go,
Even as these: and I have felt a joy,
Even as a child, in all this mighty world,
And the weird, awful mystery it held;
And taught me softly I were like the trees
And winds and flowers that come a season and die.

"O Augur, dost thou not know I am old,
With wrinkled winter writ about my face,
A trembling at the fingers and the knees,
Like some old, cunning instrument whose force
Is rattled out, fit only to be stored
Within the dusty chambers of the past,
Where wintry key-hole moanings tune in vain
The coffined mem'ries from their dusty sleep,
Where chance a heatless ray may fall at morn,
Nor startle the wainscot-gnawing, nor the dull,
Eternal presence of that lifeless past.

"O Augur, this is death, and I am fain
For the long slumber 'neath the greening grass.
For as a winter-brook beneath its ice,
My channel of life is shrunken low in me,
And life's great voices dwindle and sink afar;
And time's musician charms mine ears in vain:
For like some tree amid the forest wide,

I reared my trunk and built my tent of green,
And spread my boughs to gusty storm and sun,
And knew spring's joy and autumn's leafy pride;
And now the winter of all my days has come,
When, leafless, budless, I must lie me low;
And be a senseless mound where life will climb,
In springs to come, unconscious of my sleep.

"Nor, Augur, am I sad, nor hold desire
To lengthen out my days beyond their time;
For when the timbers of the house are rotten
The roof-tree sinks, and the old walls refuse
To keep the winters out; then comes the time
When the householder packs his goods to go.
So I will wend me where I know me not,
But down the twilight roads of easeful death,
Perchance an inn where I may find me rest.

"Yea, Augur, I had sadness in my days,

Mine evil hours as other men have had,
When night was night with scarce a morn to come,
And all the alley-ways of hope seemed stayed
With some vague stumblings, where I fained to crawl
And moan and grope and plead and feel my way.
Yea, I have had mine hours of glory too,
When life seemed all a morning stretching on
Out into sunny haze, and earth was filled
With youth and joy, and every path held hope,
Veiling the future in a glamorous mist.

"And I must say, O Augur, even now,
When I lie here upon this edge of life,
That slopes far downward to the soundless dark,
That I here feel me even as when a child
I wandered on the sunny slopes of morn,
And heard the elfin horns of faery blown
About the confines of my vision's scope.
For I hold happiness for the crumbling trunk,

Skirting the evening when the Autumn wind
Moans, querulous, along the gathering dark;
As well as for the shooting sprout that feels,
Within, the upward golden wells of Spring,
When young Pan's piping down the rosy ways
Wakens the tremulous daughters of the year.

If down some golden majesty of stairs
From some high, heart-dreamed heaven there should come
Flame-messengers, archangel-trumpeted,
And bid me fare by folds of rosy dawns,
Up to those lights eterne the angels ken;
Though down the ladders of celestial light,
Immortal invitation sought mine ears,
And beat tumultuous music in my brain,
From far-off choirs of angel harmonies;
Yet my poor heart would lean on human thoughts,
And sweetest mem'ries breed on human love,
And all my visions be of fields and flowers,

And summer brooks and winds and voices sweet,
Welling up from dreams of far-off days,
Of olden homes and faces, sweet ones loved,
Haunting from out the golden shores of youth.
Thus ever it is with age when men must die,
The phantom rivers of life must childward run,
The roads be peopled whence our hearts have come,
Who fare the ways of lonely, withered age,
The ways that lead down to the dusks of death.

"The morning roads, the golden roads of youth,
When all the future cast a majesty,
A presence as of God on field and tree,
A splendour spirit-felt, that brooded there—
The days that were, the days that are no more.

"For hearken, Augur, though a glory lies
In visions great, the human heart may build,
From out the restless longings of this life;

Not all the harpings of celestial throngs,
Tuning with spirit-songs the halls of joy,
Fabled of saints, where immortality
Hungers no more, nor dwelleth pain nor death,
Hath power to blot from out the heart of age,
Those memories divine of love and youth.
For, Augur, we are human, fleshly knit,
Aflame with all the instincts of old earth,
And she is ours and we were made for her.
We sported as babes upon her swards at morn,
Conquered her glories in our manhood's prime,
And now the even comes we backward creep
Unto her breast, like babes, to sleep at last,
Or children who assoilèd in their play;
The battles and the fears and the mad joys,
The pageants of life all hushed and overthrown,
The clamour stilled of trumpet and of drum,
The doors all sealed, the tapers flickered out,
By some black gust athwart the moors of death.

"In this dim, twilight hour of mine old age,
Your heavenly harpings reach mine ears in vain—
I, who am but a wreck of what life was—
For stronger call the voices of my youth,
And backward surge in shoals the olden loves,
The noonday struggles and the glorious hopes;
The olden spirits haunt about my bed
From out the rosy sunrise lands of eld.

"There comes the wife, belovèd, of my youth,
Making me heaven with her sainted eyes,
Within whose depths earth's love will ever shine.
Hath heaven a joy to match those memories,
Of long-gone summer nights astir with bloom,
When earth seemed new create, and life divine;
Those nights I held her first and knew her mine?
There come the babes of my maturer youth,
Their voices clamour all about my bed,
Making a music sweeter than April brooks.

Hath heaven a choir to match those earthly sounds,
That long have wandered like a morning dream,
Back to our mother-earth, where I go too?
I, who am left like some old withered tree,
The last of some dead woodland swept of time!

"I know not of the ways that lie before,
The doors of dark are sealed upon my sight,
Save that a splendour floods great heaven's floor,
Across the shapeless shadows of the night;
And all the past grows luminous and bright:
I know not of the ways that lie before,
The Eternal guides me down to nature's night.

"And, Augur, human, human to the last,
Clothed on with memories glad of love and youth,
Old Tama wanders to the dreamless dead;
Knowing no glory greater than this earth,

To sleep amid the ruins of old kings
And mighty peoples who have gone before.

"Deep in the brown earth, under the flowers and grass,
Beneath the boughs of some old spreading oak,
Beside the washings of some mighty stream,
To sleep for ever where the great hills dream;
And let the maddened march of time go by,
While over all broods the eternal sky,
Majestic, restful, as the ages pass."

STORM.

BLACK trees wind-shaken against the wild night sky,
  Deep in your glooms you cradle the voice of storms;
While far to west and south the night blows by,
  With shadowy, fleeting forms.

Under the stars with turbid, sullen mood,
  Hid in a dream of dark the river sweeps;
Where all the world by frozen field and wood,
  Chilled into numbness, sleeps.

Here dwell no pallid spirits of the day,
  But out across the icy, desolate dream,
The world of night is all storm-blown one way,
  In a loud, gusty gleam.

Soon, soon from arctic cave and bastion strong,
With elves of frost and wrinkled, sleep-eyed ghosts,
Out of the north with hornings loud and long,
Will come the grim storm-hosts.

And faster and faster on the shadowy air,
Across the phantom glimmerings of the moon,
Will fold the silences, far, chilled and bare,
In one white, mantling swoon;

And howl and shriek and moan and pass away,
Leaving the world one whited death forlorn,
When stir the slim–cold–fingered ghosts of grey
The curtains of the morn.

SIR LANCELOT.

HE rode, a king, amid the armoured knights,
The glory of day tossing on helm and shield,
And all the glory of his youth and joy,
In the strong, wine-like splendour of his face.
He rode among them, the one man of men,
Their lordliest, loveliest, he who might have been,
Because of very human breadth of love,
And his glad, winning sympathy for earth,
Greater than even Arthur under heaven.

Kindlier than the morning was his face,
Swift, like the lightning, was his eagle glance,

No bit of beauty earth had ever held,
Of child or flower or dream of woman's face,
Or noble, passing godliness of mood;
In man toward man, but garnered in his eye,
As in some mere that gathereth all earth's face,
And foldeth it in beauty to its breast.

He rode among them, Arthur's own right hand,
Arthur, whom he loved as John loved Christ,
And watched each day with joy that lofty brow
Lift up its lonely splendour, isolate,
Half god-like, o'er that serried host of spears,
And knew his love the kingliest, holiest thing,
'Twixt man and man upon this glowing earth.

So passed those days of splendour and of peace,
When all men loved his majesty and strength
And kindliness of spirit which the king,
Great Arthur, with his lofty coldness lacked.

'Twas Lancelot fought the mightiest in the lists,
And beat with thunders back the brazen shields,
And stormed the fastness of the farthest isles,
Slaying the grizzly warriors of the meres,
And winning all men's fealty and love,
And worship of fair women in the towers,
Who laid their distaffs down to watch him pass;
And made the hot blood mantle each fair cheek,
With sweet sense of his presence, till all men
Called Arthur half a god, and Lancelot
The greatest heart that beat in his great realm.

Then came that fatal day that brake his life,
When he, being sent of Arthur, all unknowing,
Saw Guinevere, like some fair flower of heaven,
As men may only see in dreams the gods
Do send to kill the common ways of earth,
And make all else but drear and dull and bleak;
Such magic she did work upon his soul,

Till Arthur, God and all the Table Round,
Were but a nebulous mist before his eyes,
In which the splendour of her beauty shone.

Henceforth the years would rise and wane and die,
And glory come and glory pass away,
And battles pass as in a troubled dream,
And Arthur be a ghost, and his knights ghosts ;—
The castles and the lists and the mad fights,
Sacking of cities, scourging of country-sides,
All dreams before his eyes ;—all, save her love.

So girded she her magic round his heart,
And meshed him in a golden mesh of love,
And marred his sense of all earth's splendour there.

But in the after-days when brake the end,
And she had fled to Glastonbury's cells,
With all the world one clamour at her sin ;

And Arthur like a storm-smit pine-tree stood,
Alone amid his kingdom's blackened ruins ;—
Then Lancelot knew his life an evil dream,
And thought him of the friendship of their youth,
And all the days that they had been together,
And "Arthur, Arthur," spake from all the meres,
And "Arthur, Arthur," moaned from days afar.
And Lancelot grieved him of his woeful sin :—
"And this the hand that smote mine Arthur down,
That brake his glory, ruined his great hope
Of one vast kingdom built on noble deeds,
And truth and peace for many days to be.
This hand that should have been his truest strength,
Next to that high honour which he held."
And all the torrents of his sorrow brake
For his own Arthur, Arthur standing lone,
Like some unriven pine that towers alone
Amid the awful ruins of a world.

And then a woeful longing smote him there,
To ride by murk and moon, by mere and waste,
To where the king made battle with his foes,
And look, unknown, upon his face, and die.

So thinking this he fled, and the queen's wraith,
A memory, in the moonlight fled with him.
But stronger with him fled his gladder youth
And all the memories of the splendid past,
Until his heart yearned for the days that were,
And that great, noble soul who fought alone.

Then coming by cock-crow and the glimmering dawn,
He reached the grey-walled castle of the land,
Where the king tarried ere he went to fight
The last dread battle of the Table Round.
And the grim sentinels who guarded there,
Thinking only of him as Arthur's friend,
And knowing not the Lancelot scandal named,

And judging by the sorrow of his face,
Deemed him some knight who came to aid the king,
And pointing past the waning beacon fires,
Said, "There he sleeps as one who hath no woes."

And Lancelot passing silent left them there,
And entering the old abbey, ('twas some ruin
Of piety and worship of past days,)
Saw in the flicker of a dying hearth,
Mingled with faint glimmering of the dawn,
The great king sleeping, where a mighty cross
Threw its dread shadow o'er his moving breast.

And Lancelot knew the same strong, god-like face
That he had worshipped in the days no more,
And all their olden gladness smote him now,
And he had wept, but that his awful sin,
That made a wall of flame betwixt them there,
Had seared the very fountains of his soul.

Whereat he moaned, "O, noble, saintly heart,
Couldst thou but know amidst thine innocent sleep,
Save for the awful sin that flames between,
That here doth stand the Lancelot of old days,
The one of all the world who loved thee most,
The joyous friend of all thy glorious youth;
O noble! god-like! Lancelot, who hath sinned
As none hath sinned against thee, now hath come
To gaze upon thy majesty and die.
O Arthur! thou great Arthur of my youth,
My sun, my joy, my glory!"
Here the king
Stirred in his sleep, and murmured, "Guinevere!"

And Lancelot feeling that an age of ages,
Hoary with all anguish of old crime
And hideous bloodshed, were now builded up
Betwixt him and the king at that one name,
Clothed with the mad despairings of his shame,

Stole like some shrunken ghost-life from that place,
To look no more upon great Arthur's face.

Then it did smite upon him he must die;
And in him the old ghost of honour woke
That he must die in battle, and go out
Where no dread sorrow could gnaw at his heart,
But all forgetting and eternal sleep.

Whereat the madness of old battle woke,
For his dread sin now burned all softness out,
And the glad kindliness of the Table Round,
And left him, shorn of all the Christian knight,
The gentle lord who only smote to save,
Or shield the helpless from the brutal stroke;
And flamed his heart there with the lust to slay,
And slaying be slain as his grim sires went out.

Then some far trumpet startled all the morn,

Trembling westward from its dewy sleep.
And with the day new battle woke the meres,
And as a wood-wolf scents the prey afar,
The noise of coming battle smote his ears,
And woke in him the fierceness of his race,
And the old pagan, joyous lust of fight.
And crying, "Farewell, Arthur, mine old youth,
Farewell, Lancelot, mine old kinder self,
Lancelot, Arthur's brother, lie there low,
Slain with the glory wherewithal you fell,
While this new Lancelot, new-bred of old time,
Before the new hope of the loftier day,
Before the reign of mercy and glad law,
Thunders in old madness forth to war."
And as in some bleak ruin of a house
Where all the sweet, home joys are ravaged out,
And some grim, evil pack hath entered in
To tear and snarl, so the old Lancelot passed.

And where he closed the battle's fiercest shock
Did hem him round, till as a mighty surf,
That clamours, thundering round some seaward tower,
Toward him the battle roared, and clanged his shield,
And fast his blade went circling in the sun,
Like some red, flaming wheel, where'er he went;
Nor cared for friend or foe, so that he slew,
And drank his cup of madness to the death.
Till those he fought with dreamed a giant earl
Of grim old days had come once more to earth,
To fight anew the battles of his youth.

But some huge islesmen of the west were there:
And they were fain to hew him down, and came
Like swift, loud storm of autumn at him there.
Then there grew clamour of the reddest fight
That ever man beheld, and all outside
Were stayed in awe to see that one man fight

With that dread host of wilding warriors there.
Nor stayed his awful brand, but left and right
Whirled he its bloody flamings in the sun,
And men went down as in October woods
Do crash the mighty trunks before the blast,
Till all were slain but one grim islesman left.
But Lancelot by this was all one stream
Of ruddy wounds, and like some fire his brain.
And, with one awful shout of battle joy,
He sent his sword-blade wheeling in the sun,
And cleft that mighty islesman to the neck;
And crying, "Arthur!" smote the earth, and died.

Then spread such terror over all the foe,
That gods did fight with them there, that they fled.
And all that day the battle moved afar,
Out to the west by distant copse and mere,
Till died the tumult, and the night came in,

With mighty hush far over all that waste.
And one by one the lonely stars came out,
And over the meres the wintry moon looked down,
Unmindful of poor Lancelot and his wounds,
His dead, lost youth, the stillness of his face,
And all that awful carnage silent there.

IN AUTUMN.

Season of the languorous gold,
  Season of the hazy drouth;
When the nights are nipt and cold,
  And the birds go calling south,
Over lakes and still lagoons,
Through the long-tranced afternoons.

Out in frosty, crimsoning woods,
  When the afternoons are sunny,
In sweet open solitudes
  Where the wild bee stores her honey,
And the bright wood-carpenter
Hammers at some dead old fir.

There the world forgets its woe,
  And the heart releases trouble,
Where the drumming partridge go,
  Trailing underneath the stubble;
While the golden afternoon
Slopes and slants and sinks too soon.

Where broad rivers, brimmed with rains,
  Wind in sinuous blue for miles
Through low, grassy meadow plains,
  Where the warm sun sifts and smiles,
And great tented elms throw
Shadows in cool depths below;—

Spirit in blue hazes clad,
  Maiden of the sunny mouth,
When the airs grow still and sad,
  And the birds are calling south,
And the far-off hills are blue,
Here I love to dream with you;

Dream the olden days of yore,
  While the wind some haunted tune
Flutes in gold-green leafy core
  Of the long-tranced afternoon;
And my heart grows still and vast
With long memories of the past.

UNABSOLVED.

A DRAMATIC MONOLOGUE.

(This poem is founded on the confession of a man who went with one of the expeditions to save Sir John Franklin's party, and who, being sent ahead, saw signs of them, but, through cowardice, was afraid to tell.)

O Father, hear my tale, then pity me,
For even God His pity hath withdrawn.
O death was dread and awful in those days!
You prate of hell and punishment to come,
And endless torments made for those who sin;
Stern priest, put down your cross and hearken me;—

I see forever a white glinting plain,
From night to night across the twinkling dark,
A world of cold and fear and dread and death,
And poor lost ones who starve and pinch and die ;—
I could have saved them—I—yes, even I.
You talk of hell! Is hell to see poor frames,
Wan, leathery cheeks, and dull, despairing eyes,
From whence a low-flamed madness ebbing out,
Goes slowly deathward, through the eerie hours,
To hear forever pitiless, icy winds
Feel in the shivering canvas of the tent,
With idle, brute curiosity nature hath,
While out around, one universe of death,
Stretches the loveless, hearthless arctic night?

This is my doom, it sitteth by my side,
And never leaves me through the desolate years.
Go, take your hell to men who never lived,
Save as, the slow world wendeth, sluggish, dull.

Even they must suffer also, poor bleak ones,
Then is your feeble comfort nothing worth.
You tell me to have hope, God will forgive,
O priest, can God forgive a sin like mine?
You say He is all-loving, did He lie
With me that night amid the eyeless dark,
And writhe with me, and whisper, "Save thyself,
That way to north lies cold and age and death,
And awful failure on men's awèd tongues,
To linger years hereafter; Southward lies
Home heat and love and sweet, blood-pulsing life—
Life, with its morns and eves and glad to-morrow,
And joy and hope for many days to be?"

Did He, I say, lie with me there that night,
And know that awful tragedy beyond,
And my poor tragedy enacted there?
Then must He feel Him since as I have felt,
And live that hideous misery in His heart.

And knowing this, I say unto thee, priest,
He could not be a God and say, forgive.
You plead my soul's salvation the one end
And aim of all my thought, then hearken, priest,
For this my sin hath made me more than wise ;—
That seems to me the one great sin I sinned
In selling all to save mine evil self.

Stay, hearken, priest, and haunt me not with hopes,
As futile as those icy-fingered winds
That stirred the canvas there that arctic night.
I bid thee hark and mumble not thy prayers
Like August bees heard in a summer room,
That drone afar, but keep them for the dead,
The dull-eared dead who sleep and heed them not.

Then hearken, priest, and learn thee of my woe,
For I have lain afar on northern nights,
By star-filled wastes, and conned it o'er and o'er,

And thought on God, and life, and many things,
And all the baffling mystery of the dark.
And I have held that awful rendezvous
Of naked self with self alone and bare,
And knew myself as men have never known;—
Have fought the duel, flashing hilt to hilt,
And blade to blade, of flesh and spirit there,
Until I lay a weak and wounded thing,
Like some poor, mangled bird the sportsman leaves,
Writhing and twisting there amid the dark.

You talk of ladders leading up to light,
Of windows bursting on the perfect day,
Of dawns grown ruddy on the blackest night,
Yea, I have groped about the muffled walls,
And beat my spirit's prison all in vain,
Only to find them shrouded fold on fold;
And still the cruel, icy stars look down,
And my dread memory stayeth with me still.

It was a strange, mad quest we went upon
To seek the living in the lifeless north.
For days and days, and long, lone, loveless nights,
We set our faces toward the arctic sky,
And threaded wastes of that lone wilderness,
Beyond the lands of summer and glad spring,
Beyond the regions kind of flower and bird,
Past glint horizons of auroral gleams,
A haunted world of winter's wizened sleep,
Where death, a giant, aged, and stark and wan,
Kept fast the entrance of those sunless caves,
Where hides the day beyond the icy seas.

Long day by day a desolation went
Where our wan faces fared, o'er all that waste;
And I was young and filled with love of life,
And fear of ugly death as some weird black,
The enemy of love and youth and joy;—
A lonely, ruined bridge at edge of night,

Fading in blackness at the outer end.
And those were cold, stern men I went with there,
Who held their lives as men do hold a gift
Not worth the keeping; men who told dread tales,
That made a madness in me of that waste
And all its hellish, lonely solitude,
And set my heart abeating for the south,
Until that awful desolation ringed
My reason round, and shrunk my fearful heart.
Yea, Father, I had saved them but for this;—
Why did they send me on alone, ahead,
Poor me, the only weak one of that band,
Who was too much of coward to show my fear?
Why did life give me that mad fear of death,
To make me selfish at the very last?
Why did God give those men into my hand,
And leave them victim to a craven fear
That walked those lonely wastes in form of man?

No, Father, take your cross, mine is a pain
That only distant ages can out-burn.
Forgiveness! No, you know not what you say;
You churchmen mumble words as charmers do,
And talk of God and love so glib and pat,
And think you reach men's souls and give them light,
When all the time my spirit is to you
A land unfound, a region far-removed,
Where walk dim ghosts of thoughts and fears and pains
You never dreamed of. What know you of souls
Like this of mine that hath girt misery's sum,
And found the black with which God veils His face.
You say the church absolves, you speak of peace,
You talk of what not even God can do
Be He but what you make Him. In my light,
And mine is light of one who knows the case,
The facts, the reasons, and hath weighed them too,
There is but one absolver, the absolved.

For I, since that far, fatal, arctic night,
Have been alone in some dread, shadowy court,
Where I was judge and guilty prisoner too.
Words, words are empty,—were life built on words,
How rich the poor would grow, the weak be strong,
The hateful loving, and the scornful weak,
The king would be a peasant, and the poor
A king in his own right; the murderer, red
From his foul guilt, would pass to God's own breast,
And all damned things, long damned of earth's consent,
And some dread law, much older far than we,
Would blossom righteous under heaven's face.

Ofttimes I think you churchmen do not feel;
You wear a mask and mumble petty hopes,
And show a righteous patronage of scorn
Toward all poor creatures who have shown life's sting;
And all the while, you of you who are men,
And not mere walking, feeding, lusting swine,

Mere mocks of human that do play a part,
Are but behind the mask a living death,
A muffled night that murmurs of the light,
A dread despair where lips have muttered hope.

Still fared we north across that frozen waste
Of icy horror ringed with awful night,
To seek the living in a world of death;
And as we fared a terror grew and grew
About my heart like madness, till I dreamed
A vague desire to flee by night and creep,
By steel-blue, windless plain and haunted wood,
And wizened shore and headland, once more south.

There as we went the days grew wan and shrunk,
And nights grew vast and weird and beautiful,
Walled with flame-glories of auroral light,
Ringing the frozen world with myriad spears
Of awful splendour there across the night.

And ever anon a shadowy, spectral pack
Of gleaming eyes and panting, lurid tongues
Haunted the lone horizon toward the south.

Then life ebbed lower in the bravest heart,
And spake the leader, "If in ten more days
We chance on nothing, then will we return,
And set our faces once more to the south."
For that dread land began to close us in,
With cold and hunger, bit at our poor limbs,
Till life grew there a feeble, flickering flame,
Amid the snows and ice-floes of that land.
Then ten days crept out shrunk and grey and wan,
With nothing but the lonely, haunted waste.
Then spake the leader, "If in five more days!"
Then parcelled out those five grey, haggard days,
While life to me grew like an ebbing tide,
That surged far out from some dread death-like strand.
And horror came upon me like the night,

That seemed to gird the world in desolate walls.
Then spake the leader, "If in three more days!"

But when the third day waned we came, at last,
Unto the shores of some dread, lonely sea,
That gloomed to north and night, and far beyond,
Where ruined straits and headlands loomed and sank,
There seemed the awful endings of the world.

Then spake the leader, "Let us go not yet,
But stay a little ere we turn us south,
Perchance, poor souls, they might be somewhere here."
And then to me, "You go, for you are young
And strong, and life throbs quickest in your veins,
And you have eyes more strong to see, for ours
Are dimmed by the dread frost-mists of this land;
And creep out there beyond yon gleaming ledge,
And bring me word of what you there may see.

And if you meet no sign of mast or sail,
Or hull or wreck, or mark of living soul,
Then we will turn our faces to the south;
For this great ocean's vastness hems us in,
And death here nightly creeps from strand to strand,
And binds with girth of black the gleaming world."

Then whispering "Madness, madness," to the dark,
I crept me fearful o'er that gleaming ledge,
And saw but night and awful gulfs of dark,
And weird ice-mountains looming desolate there,
And far beyond the vastness of that sea.
And then—O God, why died I not that hour?
Amid the gleaming floes far up that shore,
So far it seemed that man's foot scarce could go,
The certain, tapering outline of a mast,
And one small patch of rag; and then I felt
No man could ever live to reach that place,
And horror seized me of that haunted world,

That I should die there and be froze for aye,
Amid the ice-core of its awful heart.

Then crept I back the weak ghost of a life,
A miserable, shaking, coffined fear,
And spake, "I saw but ice and winds and dark,
And the dread vastness of that desolate sea."
Again he spake, "Creep out once more and look,
Perchance your sight was misled by the gleam."
And then once more I crept out on that ledge,
And saw again the night and awful dark,
And that poor beckoning mast that haunts me yet;
And as I lay those moments seemed to grow,
As men have felt in looking down long years,
And there I chose "'twixt evil and the good,"
And took the evil; then began my hell,
And back I crept with that black lie on lips,
And spake again, "I only saw the night,
And those weird mountains and the awful deep."

At that he moaned and spake, "Poor souls! Poor souls!
Then they are doomed if ever men were doomed."
Whereat a sudden, great auroral flame
Filled all the heaven, lighting wastes and sea,
And came a wondrous shock across the world,
Like sounds of far-off battle where hosts die,
As if God thundered back mine awful lie,
And I fell in a heap where all was black.

When next I lived we were full three days south,
And two had died upon that dreadful march;
Then memory came, and I went laughing mad,
But kept mine awful secret to this hour.

No, priest, you can do nothing, pain like mine
Must smoulder out in its own agony,
Till there be nought but ashes at the last.

But something 'mid the pauses of the dark
Doth teach me that I am not all alone,

For I have dreamed in my dread, maddest hour,
An awful shadow, blacker than my black,
Went ever with me. Hearken to me now:
I never felt a hand or saw a face,
I never knew a comfort more than sleep,
The winters they are only barren snows,
And age is hard, and death waits at the last.

But I have felt in some dim, shapeless way,
As memories long remembered after youth,
That back of all there is some mighty will,
Beyond the little dreams that we are here,
Beyond the misery of our days and years,
Beyond the outmost system's outmost rim,
Where wrinkled suns in awful blackness swim,
A wondrous mercy that is working still.

THE DREAMERS.

THEY lingered on the middle heights,
  Betwixt the brown earth and the heaven;
They whispered, "We are not the night's,
  But pallid children of the even."

They muttered, "We are not the day's,
  For the old struggle and endeavor,
The rugged and unquiet ways,
  Are dead and driven past for ever."

They dreamed upon the cricket's tune,
  The winds that stirred the withered grasses:
But never saw the blood-red moon,
  That lit the spectre mountain-passes.

They sat and marked the brooklet steal
  In smoke-mist o'er its silvered surges:
But marked not, with its peal on peal,
  The storm that swept the granite gorges.

They dreamed the shimmer and the shade,
  And sought in pools for haunted faces:
Nor heard again the cannonade,
  In dreams from earth's old battle-places.

They spake, "The ages all are dead,
  The strife, the struggle and the glory;
We are the silences that wed,
  Betwixt the story and the story.

"We are the little winds that moan
  Between the woodlands and the meadows,
We are the ghosted leaves, wind-blown
  Across the gust-light and the shadows."

Then came a soul across those lands,
  Whose face was all one glad, rapt wonder;
And spake: "The skies are ribbed with bands
  Of fire, and heaven all racked with thunder.

"Climb up and see the glory spread,
  High over cliff and 'scarpment yawning:
The night is past, the dark is dead,
  Behold the triumph of the dawning!"

Then laughed they with a wistful scorn,
  "You are a ghost, a long-dead vision;
You passed by ages ere was born
  This twilight of the days elysian.

"There is no hope, there is no strife,
  But only haunted hearts that hunger,
About a dead, scarce dreamed-of life,
  Old ages when the earth was younger."

Then came by one in mad distress,
  "Haste, haste, below where strong arms weaken,
The fighting ones grow less and less!
  Great cities of the world are taken!

"Dread evil rolls by like a flood,
  Men's bones beneath his surges whiten,
Go where the ages mark in blood
  The footsteps that their days enlighten."

Still they but heard, discordant mirth,
  The thin winds through the dead stalks rattle;
While out from far-off haunts of earth,
  There smote the mighty sound of battle.

Now there was heard an awful cry,
  Despair that rended heaven asunder,
White pauses when a cause would die,
  Where love was lost and souls went under.

The while these feebly dreamed and talked,
  Betwixt the brown earth and the heaven,
Faint ghosts of men who breathed and walked,
  But deader than the dead ones even.

And out there on the middle height,
  They sought in pools for haunted faces,
Nor heard the cry across the night,
  That swept from earth's dread battle-places.

THE MOTHER.

THE MOTHER.

I.

It was April, blossoming spring,
They buried me, when the birds did sing;

Earth, in clammy wedging earth,
They banked my bed with a black, damp girth.

Under the damp and under the mould,
I kenned my breasts were clammy and cold.

Out from the red beams, slanting and bright,
I kenned my cheeks were sunken and white.

I was a dream, and the world was a dream,
And yet I kenned all things that seem.

I was a dream, and the world was a dream,
But you cannot bury a red sunbeam.

For though in the under-grave's doom-night
I lay all silent and stark and white,

Yet over my head I seemed to know
The murmurous moods of wind and snow,

The snows that wasted, the winds that blew,
The rays that slanted, the clouds that drew

The water-ghosts up from lakes below,
And the little flower-souls in earth that grow.

Under earth, in the grave's stark night,
I felt the stars and the moon's pale light.

I felt the winds of ocean and land
That whispered the blossoms soft and bland.

Though they had buried me dark and low,
My soul with the season's seemed to grow.

II.

I was a bride in my sickness sore,
I was a bride nine months and more.

From throes of pain they buried me low,
For death had finished a mother's woe.

But under the sod, in the grave's dread doom,
I dreamed of my baby in glimmer and gloom.

I dreamed of my babe, and I kenned that his rest
Was broken in wailings on my dead breast.

I dreamed that a rose-leaf hand did cling:
Oh, you cannot bury a mother in spring.

When the winds are soft and the blossoms are red
She could not sleep in her cold earth-bed.

I dreamed of my babe for a day and a night,
And then I rose in my grave-clothes white.

I rose like a flower from my damp earth-bed
To the world of sorrowing overhead.

Men would have called me a thing of harm,
But dreams of my babe made me rosy and warm.

I felt my breasts swell under my shroud;
No stars shone white, no winds were loud;

But I stole me past the graveyard wall,
For the voice of my baby seemed to call;

And I kenned me a voice, though my lips were dumb:
Hush, baby, hush! for mother is come.

I passed the streets to my husband's home;
The chamber stairs in a dream I clomb;

I heard the sound of each sleeper's breath,
Light waves that break on the shores of death.

I listened a space at my chamber door,
Then stole like a moon-ray over its floor.

My babe was asleep on a stranger arm,
"O baby, my baby, the grave is so warm,

"Though dark and so deep, for mother is there!
O come with me from the pain and care!

"O come with me from the anguish of earth,
Where the bed is banked with a blossoming girth,

"Where the pillow is soft and the rest is long,
And mother will croon you a slumber-song,

"A slumber-song that will charm your eyes
To a sleep that never in earth-song lies!

"The loves of earth your being can spare,
But never the grave, for mother is there."

I nestled him soft to my throbbing breast,
And stole me back to my long, long rest.

And here I lie with him under the stars,
Dead to earth, its peace and its wars;

Dead to its hates, its hopes, and its harms,
So long as he cradles up soft in my arms.

And heaven may open its shimmering doors,
And saints make music on pearly floors,

And hell may yawn to its infinite sea,
But they never can take my baby from me.

For so much a part of my soul he hath grown
That God doth know of it high on His throne.

And here I lie with him under the flowers
That sun-winds rock through the billowy hours,

With the night-airs that steal from the murmuring sea,
Bringing sweet peace to my baby and me.

DUSK.

Down by the shore at even, when the waves
Lap lightly on the reedy rims, and soft,
One trembling star, a blossom, flames aloft,
Where the sunk sun the western heaven laves
With lowest tides of day; the tired world craves
For the great night, that cometh brooding in,
With draught of healing over earth's far din,
And blessed rest that recreates and saves.

Far in the breathing woods the whip-poor-will
Reiterates his plaintive note; and hark!
A dusky night-hawk whirrs athwart the dark,
Haunting the shadows, till in silvern swoon,
Hunted by her own spirit, strange and still,
Over the waters comes the wan, white moon.

OUT OF POMPEII.

SHE lay, face downward, on her bended arm,
  In this her new, sweet dream of human bliss,
Her heart within her fearful, fluttering, warm,
  Her lips yet pained with love's first timorous kiss.
She did not note the darkening afternoon,
  She did not mark the lowering of the sky
O'er that great city. Earth had given its boon
  Unto her lips, love touched her and passed by.

In one dread moment all the sky grew dark,
  The hideous rain, the panic, the red rout,
Where love lost love, and all the world might mark
  The city overwhelmed, blotted out

Without one cry, so quick oblivion came,
  And life passed to the black where all forget;
But she,—we know not of her house or name,—
  In love's sweet musings doth lie dreaming yet.

The dread hell passed, the ruined world grew still,
  And the great city passed to nothingness:
The ages went and mankind worked its will.
  Then men stood still amid the centuries' press,
And in the ash-hid ruins opened bare,
  As she lay down in her shamed loveliness,
Sculptured and frozen, late they found her there,
  Image of love 'mid all that hideousness.

Her head, face downward, on her bended arm,
  Her single robe that showed her shapely form,
Her wondrous fate love keeps divinely warm
  Over the centuries, past the slaying storm,

The heart can read in writings time hath left,
  That linger still through death's oblivion;
And in this waste of life and light bereft,
  She brings again a beauty that had gone.

And if there be a day when all shall wake,
  As dreams the hoping, doubting human heart,
The dim forgetfulness of death will break
  For her as one who sleeps with lips apart;
And did God call her suddenly, I know
  She'd wake as morning wakened by the thrush,
Feel that red kiss across the centuries glow,
  And make all heaven rosier by her blush.

MORNING ON THE SHORE.

THE lake is blue with morning; and the sky
  Sweet, clear, and burnished as an orient pearl.
  High in its vastness, scream and skim and whirl
White gull-flocks where the gleaming beaches die
Into dim distance, where great marshes lie.
  Far in ashore the woods are warm with dreams,
  The dew-wet road in ruddy sunlight gleams,
The sweet, cool earth, the clear blue heaven on high.

Across the morn a carolling school-boy goes,
Filling the world with youth to heaven's stair;
  Some chattering squirrel answers from his tree;
But down beyond the headland, where ice-floes
Are great in winter, pleading in mute prayer,
  A dead, drowned face stares up immutably.

PAN THE FALLEN.

He wandered into the market
  With pipes and goatish hoof;
He wandered in a grotesque shape,
  And no one stood aloof.
For the children crowded round him,
  The wives and greybeards, too,
To crack their jokes and have their mirth,
  And see what Pan would do.

The Pan he was they knew him,
  Part man, but mostly beast,
Who drank, and lied, and snatched what bones
  Men threw him from their feast;

Who seemed in sin so merry,
  So careless in his woe,
That men despised, scarce pitied him,
  And still would have it so.

He swelled his pipes and thrilled them,
  And drew the silent tear;
He made the gravest clack with mirth
  By his sardonic leer.
He blew his pipes full sweetly
  At their amused demands,
And caught the scornful, earth-flung pence
  That fell from careless hands.

He saw the mob's derision,
  And took it kindly, too,
And when an epithet was flung,
  A coarser back he threw;
But under all the masking
  Of a brute, unseemly part,

I looked, and saw a wounded soul,
  And a god-like, breaking heart.

And back of the elfin music,
  The burlesque, clownish play,
I knew a wail that the weird pipes made,
  A look that was far awáy,—
A gaze into some far heaven
  Whence a soul had fallen down;
But the mob only saw the grotesque beast
  And the antics of the clown.

For scant-flung pence he paid them
  With mirth and elfin play,
Till, tired for a time of his antics queer,
  They passed and went their way;
Then there in the empty market
  He ate his scanty crust,
And, tired face turned to heaven, down
  He laid him in the dust.

And over his wild, strange features
  A softer light there fell,
And on his worn, earth-driven heart
  A peace ineffable.
And the moon rose over the market,
  But Pan the beast was dead;
While Pan the god lay silent there,
  With his strange, distorted head.

And the people, when they found him,
  Stood still with awesome fear.
No more they saw the beast's rude hoof,
  The furtive, clownish leer;
But the lightest in that audience
  Went silent from the place,
For they knew the look of a god released
  That shone from his dead face.

THE CLOUD MAIDEN.

SHE folds about her shining form
The azure mantle of the skies,
And sendeth earthward, kind and warm,
The gentle lightnings of her eyes.

She drifts in gold and azure furled,
This sweet, mad demon of the air,
Her love the kindliest in God's world,
But when she hates, her hate beware.

She floats at heaven's gates when dawn
Spills in the east his rosy fires,
She comes at eve when day is gone,
Reviving all his dead desires.

All essences came to her birth,
  The dews that drop, the airs that run;
She is the offspring of the earth,
  The daughter of the flaming sun.

She is most kind to everything,
  The thirsty grasses, buds and flowers,
And to the poet's heart doth bring
  Thought-blossoms from her skyey bowers.

The spirits of the upper space,
  The swart, black genies under sea,
All for the glamour of her face,
  Are hers through all eternity.

They love, they hate, they wake, they sleep,
  Just as she waves her shining hands;
Just as she wills, the deepest deep
  Is stirred to do her heart's commands.

But when her mad, weird mood comes on
  Her demons all go mad with her;
They shout the churning seas upon,
  And wrap the heavens in a blur.

She trails a ragged witch in grey
  Across the heaven's wind-blown bars,
And in her ashen folds away
  She hides the shuddering moon and stars.

And when she winds her ebon cloak,
  And leaps red levin from her eyes,
She rends the century-ringèd oak,
  And laughs in thunder as it lies.

THE WERE-WOLVES.

THEY hasten, still they hasten,
  From the even to the dawn;
And their tired eyes gleam and glis'en
  Under north skies white and wan.
Each panter in the darkness
  Is a demon-haunted soul,
The shadowy, phantom were-wolves,
  Who circle round the Pole.

Their tongues are crimson flaming,
  Their haunted blue eyes gleam,
And they strain them to the utmost
  O'er frozen lake and stream;

Their cry one note of agony,
  That is neither yelp nor bark,
These panters of the northern waste,
  Who hound them to the dark.

You may hear their hurried breathing,
  You may see their fleeting forms,
At the pallid polar midnight,
  When the north is gathering storms;
When the arctic frosts are flaming,
  And the ice-field thunders roll;
These demon-haunted were-wolves,
  Who circle round the Pole.

They hasten, still they hasten,
  Across the northern night,
Filled with a frighted madness,
  A horror of the light;

Forever and forever,
  Like leaves before the wind,
They leave the wan, white gleaming
  Of the dawning far behind.

Their only peace is darkness,
  Their rest to hasten on
Into the heart of midnight,
  Forever from the dawn.
Across far phantom ice-floes
  The eye of night may mark
These horror-haunted were-wolves
  Who hound them to the dark.

All through this hideous journey,
  They are the souls of men
Who in the far dark-ages
  Made Europe one black fen.

They fled from courts and convents,
  And bound their mortal dust
With demon wolfish girdles
  Of human hate and lust.

These who could have been god-like,
  Chose, each a loathsome beast,
Amid the heart's foul graveyards,
  On putrid thoughts to feast;
But the great God who made them
  Gave each a human soul,
And so 'mid night forever
  They circle round the Pole.

A praying for the blackness,
  A longing for the night,
For each is doomed forever
  By a horror of the light;

And far in the heart of midnight,
  Where their shadowy flight is hurled,
They feel with pain the dawning
  That creeps in round the world.

Under the northern midnight,
  The white, glint ice upon,
They hasten, still they hasten,
  With their horror of the dawn;
Forever and forever,
  Into the night away
They hasten, still they hasten
  Unto the judgment day.

BELATED.

The year drifts sadly back this way,
  With Autumn's grief and pain;
But with the red leaf and the gold
  She ne'er will come again.

This world hath its weird beauteousness,
  That youth in music stirs,
But time will ne'er bring back to earth
  The beauty that was hers.

You could not call a red leaf God's
  If she were not God's too;
A light fell on such eyes and lips
  Man never more will woo.

When her smile went the day's went too,
  Night, when she closed her eyes,
Lost half its glory. When she woke
  Earth changed to paradise.

She looked so peaceful in her sleep
  When they laid her to her rest,
I could not help but think upon
  An infant at the breast.

She looked so like to one who'd wake
  This side the break of dawn;
I grudged the very earth they heaped
  Her snow-like breast upon.

I hear her low voice calling soft,
  Her footstep at the doors;
I wake up in the dead of night,
  And walk the wintry floors.

I see her croon her babe to sleep,
  Athwart the moonlight now,
Her wealth of golden hair that fell
  Across her gentle brow.

I often walk at death of day,
  Amid the sunset firs,
And dream the world will no more know
  The beauty that was hers.

I wonder in some far-off state,
  If love can conquer death,
Will I know her and she know me,
  As when she drew life's breath?

And will she stand at some flame-gate,
  And wait and watch for me,
And fall upon my breast and weep
  With joy my face to see?

And bring the little ones around
  To climb to father's arms;
While her sweet face, the face of yore,
  To mother-beauty warms?

And we go, laughing, weeping, through
  Some gate of crystal dome,
While love grows God-like more and more,
  To greet the wanderer home.

AN AUGUST REVERIE.

AN AUGUST REVERIE.

THERE is an autumn sense subdues the air,
  Though it is August and the season still
A part of summer, and the woodlands fair.
  I hear it in the humming of the mill,
I feel it in the rustling of the trees,
That scarcely shiver in the passing breeze.

'Tis but a touch of Winter ere his time,
  A presaging of sleep and icy death,
When skies are rich and fields are in their prime,
  And heaven and earth commingle in a breath:—
When hazy airs are stirred with gossamer wings,
And in shorn fields the shrill cicada sings.

So comes the slow revolving of the year,
  The glory of nature ripening to decay,
When in those paths by which, through loves austere,
  All men and beasts and blossoms find their way,
By steady easings of the spirit's dream,
From sunlight past the pallid starlight's beam.

Nor should the spirit sorrow as it passes,
  Declining slowly by the heights it came;
We are but brothers to the birds and grasses,
  In our brief coming and our end the same:—
And though we glory, god-like in our day,
Perchance some kindred law their lives obey.

There are a thousand beauties gathered round,
  The sounds of waters falling over-night,
The morning scents that steamed from the fresh ground,
  The hair-like streaming of the morning light

Through early mists and dim, wet woods where brooks
Chatter, half-seen, down under mossy nooks.

The ragged daisy starring all the fields,
  The buttercup abrim with pallid gold,
The thistle and burr-flowers hedged with prickly shields,
  All common weeds the draggled pastures hold,
With shrivelled pods and leaves, are kin to me,
Like-heirs of earth and her maturity.

They speak a silent speech that is their own,
  These wise and gentle teachers of the grass;
And when their brief and common days are flown,
  A certain beauty from the year doth pass :—
A beauty of whose light no eye can tell,
Save that it went; and my heart knew it well.

I may not know each plant as some men know them,
  Like children gather beasts and birds to tame;

But I went 'mid them as the winds that blow them,
  From childhood's hour, and loved without a name:—
There is more of beauty in a field of weeds,
Than in all blooms the hot-house garden breeds.

For they are nature's children, in their faces
  I see that sweet obedience to the sky
That marks these dwellers of the wilding places,
  Who with the season's being live and die;
Knowing no love but of the wind and sun,
Who still are nature's when their life is done.

They are a part of all the haze-filled hours,
  The happy, happy world all drenched with light,
The far-off, chiming click-clack of the mowers,
  And yon blue hills whose mists elude my sight,
And they to me will ever bring in dreams
Far mist-clad heights and brimming rain-fed streams.

In this dream August air, whose ripened leaf,
  Pausing before it puts death's glories on,
Deepens its green, and the half-garnered sheaf
  Gladdens the haze-filled sunlight; love hath gone
Beyond the material, trembling like a star,
To those sure heights where all thought's glories are.

And Thought, that is the greatness of this earth,
  And man's most inmost being, soars and soars,
Beyond the eye's horizon's outmost girth,
  Garners all beauty, on all mystery pores:—
Like some ethereal fountain in its flow,
Finds heavens where the senses may not go.

IN THE SPRING FIELDS.

THERE dwells a spirit in the budding year—
As motherhood doth beautify the face—
That even lends these barren glebes a grace,
And fills grey hours with beauty that were drear
And bleak when the loud, storming March was here:
A glamour that the thrilled heart dimly traces
In swelling boughs and soft, wet, windy spaces,
And sunlands where the chattering birds make cheer.

I thread the uplands where the wind's footfalls
Stir leaves in gusty hollows, autumn's urns.
Seaward the river's shining breast expands,
High in the windy pines a lone crow calls,
And far below some patient ploughman turns
His great black furrow over steaming lands.

IN A JUNE NIGHT.

SEE how the luminous night hath drawn around
The curtains of her majesty, and o'er
The far-heard, murmurous sounds of earthly life
Hath dropped the mantle of her misty sleep,
That spreads itself and folds the corners in
Of darkness round this hid rim of the world.

O Beauty, thou art never half so rare
And restful to the spirit as when thou
Dost throne thyself amid the dome of night,
The deep blue zenith that is scarcely blue,
Where darkness scarce takes color, and the arch
Of heaven glows with myriad misty fires,

That move like spirits in majestic space,
And fill with inward music the great void
That tunes itself to match the seraphim,
And lifts the heart of man to higher planes
Of strength and greatness. I have seen thy face
At kindling morning or at dreamy eve,
Or mid the pauses of a summer noon,
When thou didst glass thee in a woodland pool,
Where sound was far, and all the world a dream.

And I have hunted thee down autumn lanes,
Dream-avenues of mists and ruddy fires,
Past the complainings of the thoughtful wind,
That in the under-heart of woodlands moaned,
And jargoned memories of the haunted past.

Or I have seen thy presence in the storm,
The quick, mad muttering of the thunder-cloud,
That zigzagged all the ashen fields with red,

Followed by the sudden rushing rain,
That roared the roof-tops and the window-panes,
And threshed the grain-fields and the garden flowers,
And flooded the dusty roads with pools and streams,
While all the heaven brimmed with fire and rain:
Then darkened past and left the summer sky
As stainless as the blue eye of a child;
And all the world alit with trembling gems,
Beneath the sunlight and the cooling air.

Or I have seen thine awfuller majesty
In mad November, when his muffled storms,
Loud-tongued and mighty, racked the skeleton woods,
And roared and surged amid the branchy tops,
Like some far surf of ocean on his shore,
Hounding the frosts from their still fastness there.
Or in the frosty silence of deep snows
And long-drawn, silent nights of weeping winds,

Crooning a tune amid the skeleton trees;
Thy spirit hath made music in my heart.

But thou art draped in all thy glow, supreme,
Here in the luminous dream of this June night,
When all the heaven's roof doth seem to rise
And lift and lift in endless floors of light;
Glad wells of glory, infinities of space,
Jewelled with wheeling systems, circling round
In silvered journeyings o'er the seas of night.

Down under here the mother-earth is still
And shadowed, save that for a spirit-wind
That whispers in a voice, so low, so low,
That scarcely makes a rustle in grasses heard;
Or low, cool breathings of the forest edge.
Down near by in the covert thicket hid,
Like molten silver or white moving mist,
Could you but see it, hark, a gurgling brook,

That goes so silvern, silvern, down its stones,
Blithely, like the sweet notes of a song,
Tenderly, from dripping stone to stone,
Filling the night with drowsèd melody.

This is a clime where spirits only dwell,
And man knows he is god-like; love finds wings,
And wisdom spans existence. Under here
My soul doth find the infinite, glad rest,
And all my heart grows kindred with the stars.

HARVEST SLUMBER SONG.

SLEEP, little baby, sleep, sleep, sleep,
Red is the moon in the night's still deep,
White are the stars with their silver wings
Folded in dreamings of beautiful things,
And over their cradle the night wind sings,
Sleep, little baby, sleep, sleep, sleep.

Soft in the lap of the mother night
The wee baby stars, all glowing and bright,
Flutter their silver wings and crow
To the watchful winds that kiss as they blow
Round the air-cradle that swings so low
Down in the lap of the mother night.

Sleep, little baby, sleep, sleep, sleep,
Red is the moon in the night's still deep,
And the wee baby stars are all folded and kissed
In a luminous cradle of silver mist;
And if ever they waken the winds cry, Whist,
Sleep, little baby, sleep, sleep, sleep.

AUTUMN.

SEASON of languorous gold and hazy drouth,
  Of nature's beauty ripened to the core,
When over fens far-calling birds wing south,
  Filling the air with lonesome dreams of yore,
  And memories that haunt but come no more;
Maiden of veilèd eyes and sunny mouth,
Dreaming between hushed heat and frosted lands;
With fire-mists in thine eyes, and red leaves in thy hands.

Spirit of Autumn, siren of all the year,
  Who dost my soul with glamouries entwine;
As some old trunk, deep in the forest drear,
  Is gloried by some crimson, clinging vine;

So thou dost fill my heart with haunted wine,
When in the still, glad days by uplands sere,
With slow-drawn pace, I seek thy slumberous moods,
In thy hushed, dreamy haunts of fields and skies and
woods.

How often in the still, rich frosted days,
Down the slow hours of some tranced afternoon,
Have my feet wandered in a mad, sweet maze,
Hunting the wind that, like some haunting tune,
Peopled with memories all the great, gold swoon
Of rustling woodlands, streams and leafy ways,
Ever eluding, fluting, sweet, before
Fading to rest at last in gold-green leafy core.

Far out beside some great, hill-cradled stream,
Winding along in sinuous blue for miles,
By tented elms, in fields that sleep and dream,

Low marsh-lands where the warm sun slopes and
smiles,
Where through the haze the harsh grasshopper files
His rasping note. The pallid asters gleam,
And golden rod flames in the smoky light,
While far, blue fading hills in mists elude my sight.

Or out in maple woods where companies
Of sombre trunks lift the soft light between,
And little sunbeams steal with ruddy eyes,
Sifting adown the canopies of green;
Spirit of sadness, here you move unseen
Down tented avenues where the long light lies
From morn till even, through the silent hours,
Where over all the day frets through in sunny showers.

On silent nights, grey mists creep near the ground,
And airs are keen and stars grow sharp and clear,

And phantom frosts steal in and make no sound
Down the long, haunted river, bleak and drear,
Biting with death the sedges dank and sere,
And ever the wan moon rises large and round
Over the woodlands, flooding with icèd dream
The far-hushed, ghostly face of wood and field and stream.

On frosty mornings in the crimsoning woods;
Or where the long, low grassy meadows shine,
Wimpling and steaming out through hazy moods
Of dewy glories to the far sky-line;
And pearly brooks, a company divine,
Go, softly chattering, under smoky hoods;
I love to walk abroad and con with you
Dream thoughts that are most sad and beautiful and true.

TO THE RIDEAU RIVER.

You wander, shining, down all happy places,
You kiss the over-airs with misty lips,
You mirror in your depths all earth's glad faces,
While low to you in love the heaven dips.

About you gather all the loves of summer,
You sing glad morning and tired eve to sleep,
Lifting your cooling cup to each new comer,
Till hearts grow strong where life was at its neap.

O river, glad and bounteous in your singing,
So restful and continuous night and day,
You seem to voice the feathered creatures winging,
And little children in their joyous play.

You bring to earth a long-lost, olden beauty,
  When filling summer with your slumb'rous sound;
You banish stress and strife and barren duty,
  Brimming with joyance all the world around.

I gaze upon your shining face at morning,
  When woods are fresh and dews are on the grass;
And light and love, the night and darkness scorning,
  Fill earth with song from each bush where I pass.

I gaze upon your misty face at even,
  Athwart the golden chambers of the west,
When ever-changing glories of the heaven
  Build up a broken splendour in thy breast.

And when the misty moon, in pallid glory,
  Glimmers across the ghost-lagoons of night,
Within your breast there haunts the spectre story
  Of her pale loves and dreams in tremulous light.

Across the peace of all the night's great healing,
  Beneath the silence of the dark's hushed deep,
A phosphorescent, ghostly spirit stealing,
  You softly slide, a sleep within a sleep.

You slip and shine by boughs that bend to kiss you,
  You dream by curvèd banks of shimmering green;
And where you swerve the alien meadows miss you,
  But happy are the banks you glide between.

You drift, a solace to the great woods under,
  Wimpling wide in many a watery moon;
And when you sing, the hours, in soft-eyed wonder,
  Lean, finger on lip, entrancèd by your tune.

Out by dim, hazy shores, in reedy shallows,
  The drowsy cattle sun them in the heat;
And, far from woody slopes and ragged fallows,
  A lazy wind goes loitering in the wheat.

You fill the summer with your magic chanting
  Your sleepy music out by field and fell;
And spirits elusive in your bosom haunting,
  Sleep like the genie in the Arabian well.

In low green capes, by country ways descending,
  Where your tides wind by many a braided shore,
The great cool elms, the heaven and water blending,
  Mirror their ghosts within thy shimmering floor.

By pebbly shoals whereon your tides are driven,
  In silvery surge and far-heard slumb'rous song,
Your sleeping shores and the white hosts of heaven
  Hearken your tender droppings all night long.

Where out along the dusk, all white-mist laden,
  You cradle deep in wells of azure light,—
Like to the virgin dreams of some sweet maiden,—
  In your glad breast the million stars of night.

The great, hot city calls with its loud clamour,
  Unrecked, unheeded here at night or noon;
Faint, far-away breaks in its baleful glamour
  'Mid wildernesses 'neath the sun and moon;

Across your silver bars whereby you glisten,
  Oblivious of the throe of earth's wild mart,
You leap and sing, and then you lie and listen,
  As if to hear the throbbing of your heart.

O happy, happy stream, drift softly, slowly,
  Through sunlit hours in musical, sweet ways,
Thine are the haunts all unprofaned and holy,
  Far from earth's life and all its maddened maze.

Thine is the peace, the glory and the splendour,
  That mother nature gives unto her own;
Thine are the dreams, all glad, elusive, tender,
  With which she veils herself, remote, alone.

When she withdraws herself from man's rude peering
  Into the virgin secrets of her heart,
Out from the realms of hate and doubt and fearing,
  Unto her life of dreams, shut out, apart.

Where no soul reaches save some kindred spirit,
  Some late-born satyr çaged in human form,
Some child of that old order who inherit
  The haunting beauty of the ages' storm.

Strange children, smitten with the dream of seeing
  The glory that lies under this mad life;
The folds of midnight back of all this being,
  The majesty of sleep behind the strife.

Even I am one of those, glad, haunted river,
  A soul belated from the great ones gone;
Wandering here at twilight, doomèd ever
  Mid alien days and dreams to wander on;

Hearing by grove and stream old voices calling
  In holy runes of earth's primeval tongue;
Mad music in the air about me falling,
  Out of the ages when the earth was young.

For I am not of all this weird mob, thronging
  The streets of mad to-day, the world's dread throe;
I walk apart all hungered with a longing
  For some departed, mighty long ago.

Unfettered child of nature's mirth and gladness,
  Sing, sing and drift by field and country way;
Fill earth and men with thy divine, sweet madness,
  With glad contentment gird both night and day:

Till even I, with every sad-eyed brother,
  Pausing amid the felon cares of life,
Fare back through thee to earth our great kind mother,
  Forgetting failure, bitterness and strife.

And care and pain one troublous dream dissolving,
  Across the splendour of thy misty bars ;
We only know the glorious day revolving,
  Night's majesty, and her eternal stars.

IN THE AUGUST FIELDS.

A SOFT, blue vapour films the fields and woods;
Through shining heats, a thread, the roadway runs;
Far out in smoke, the white day sleeps and suns,
And faint and dim the city's jar intrudes
Across these realms of summer's solitudes,
Walled in by azure of the horizon's rim:
Where the great sky, all arched and blurred and dim,
About this drowse and dreaming bends and broods.

Near in the heat a locust lilts and files,
A sheep-bell tinkles down along the grass,
And out by hill and valley, miles on miles,
With summer's breath across its face half blurred,
Cradling this silence all unjarred, unstirred,
The river holds the whole world like a glass.

IN THE STRENGTH OF THE MORNING.

I STAND upon the morning's rim,
And all life's dream within me thrills;
I am the cup whose beaded brim
The wine of living holds or spills:
I stand upon the morning's rim,
When day grows rose and night is dim.

There comes a freshness from the floor
Of ocean and the night-bathed land;
A spirit swings each roseate door
With winnowing wings and odours bland:
Rose flames enkindle heaven's floor,
And the grey mists are night no more.

I stand upon the morning's verge,
  And feel the glorious waking world;
Afar I hear life's thundering surge
  On morning's beaches maddening hurled,
In flame-tinged beauty, where the verge
Of ocean sings melodious dirge.

I stand at morning's rim and know
  That all this dream of earth and sea,
These clouds and dreamy fields below,
  This azure sphere, were made for me:
That all are mine that morn doth know,
The airs that brood, the blades that grow.

I walk in fields knee-deep in grass,
  Where heavenward elms spread their arms;
I dream the airs of morning pass,
  With voices from a hundred farms:
The bobolink rises from the grass,
Brim with the melody morning has.

I wander by the shade of woods,
  In roadways brown and wet with dew—
The great cool, leafy solitudes ;
  My heart grows great and lonely too,
With the large wisdom of the woods,
Full of the morning's haunted moods.

The world grows faint and far away,
  As morning grows a dream at noon ;
Here the great silences do pray,
  With spread arms in a voiceless swoon :
The fields gleam out and far away
Across the hum and hush of day.

I breathe life's airs and feel my heart
  Leap into being, like a brook
That from a mountain crag doth start,
  And falls in snowy thunders shook :
So all earth's glories in my heart
Surge outward, nature's counterpart.

The over-moving fields of blue,
  They are the dreams that God hath spread,
With dews and fires of morning too,
  Far out around above my head:
I feel their deep, far-lifting blue,
Shot with the morning's radiance through.

Here in the brooding earth I dream
  The great, high visions of the soul;
Strong like the swerved tide of the stream,
  Broad like the morn's unbroken whole:
Majestic hopes of life I dream,
Such visions great a god might deem.

So clear the river's eye is clear,
  So strong and fresh the smell of earth,
So gladly heaven hovers near,
  Great thoughts could scarcely fail of birth:
The very soul grows crystal clear,
Like some pure, spring-fed mountain mere.

Out here across this wind-blown land,
  Where all is great and glad and new,
I feel my spirit's wings expand
  Like eagle's under heaven's blue:
Great with the strength of sea and land,
I grasp life's problems in my hand.

Back downward to the world I go,
  Filled with the glory of earth's light;
No demon dread can overthrow,
  No dreams of evil e'er affright:
To battle with my fate I go,
Across the days of strife and woe.

No frosts of wintry age can chill,
  No deeps of midnight swirl me down;
The fires of Spring my being thrill,
  The dreams of morning fence me round:
By blue, blue brooks that never chill,
I climb for aye a summer hill.

I climb and listen to a song,
  Sung by a bird at Summer's dawn,
A song that holds no note of wrong,
  Dreamed from the world where love hath gone:
I listen, listen till that song,
Like God's voice, makes the years more strong.

AN OCTOBER EVENING.

THE woods are haggard and lonely,
The skies are hooded for snow,
The moon is cold in Heaven,
And the grasses are sere below.

The bearded swamps are breathing
A mist from meres afar,
And grimly the Great Bear circles
Under the pale Pole Star.

There is never a voice in Heaven,
Nor ever a sound on earth,
Where the spectres of winter are rising
Over the night's wan girth.

There is slumber and death in the silence,
  There is hate in the winds so keen;
And the flash of the north's great sword-blade
  Circles its cruel sheen.

The world grows agèd and wintry,
  Love's face peakèd and white;
And death is kind to the tired ones
  Who sleep in the north to-night.

DECEMBER.

Blowest thou in again, thou bleak December,
Comest thou back with bearded, icy sheen,
Lone hours that make the saddened heart remember
The flower of life, the sweetness that hath been:
Grey, chilly skies, wild winds that fray and fret,
Bring me kind peace or bid the heart forget.

Comest thou in with thy rude, kindly bluster,
The wintry glow of fagots on pale fires;
Thy lonesome woodlands in a ragged cluster
About the earth's shrunk edge, with dreary spires
Of tree-tops loomed athwart the chilly sky;
Where late the low night-wind went haunting by.

I love thee, Month, for all thy cold north blowing;
I greet thee, friend, for all thy frosty mood;
With mantling blood I meet thy slanted snowing,
O'er withered field or by the leafless wood,
Whose damp earth-floors with rain-bleached leaves are stained,
And frosty nuts that rich November rained.

Men call thee rude, but thou art soft and gentle,
Thy voice is loud, but oh, thy heart is kind,
Who coverest shivering earth with thy soft mantle,
To shield the grasses from the cruel wind:
And the sweet buds in brown earth laid away,
Thou tendest for thy gentle sister May.

When haggard cold hath nipped the hills and meadows,
And chilly mornings lift from pallid skies,
And chimney smoke to earthward sendeth shadows;
'Tis then I seek thine icèd glamouries,
In lonely ways of wood, and watery field,
Which thou hast silvered with a frosty shield.

O'er ways of the wind's moods of fitful wandering,
  Or querulous moanings by some hillside bare,
Naked of snows, where Heaven's largesse squandering,
  The night had built snow-turrets here and there,
Heaping the hollows, cloaking stumps and trees
With wintry coat of ermine draperies.

Or 'neath gaunt aisles of sombre woodlands crooning,
  Like gray old crones, some sad December song,
Or barren trees like aged harpers tuning
  Their withered instruments, an eerie throng,
Bright icicles from each white, branchy beard,
Stand waiting for the dying old year's weird.

So I have roamed with thee, thou grey December,
  Through all thy sheeted nights and withered days;
And dreamed beneath thy chillèd ice and ember,
  The secret thoughts of Nature's hidden ways:
How under all thy storm and maddened moods,
Thou barest her message to the fields and woods.

PREMONITIONS.

In the winter wan and white,
When the days grow long and bright,
And the sun grows warm and hot
In each southward sheltered spot
Back of fences, under hills;
Then my brain with fancy fills,
Then my heart grows young again
Through the days that wax and wane.

In the morning when I wake,
Something all my heart doth take
Captive with a secret thrill
Toward the young year's waking will;

When I feel the sun behind
My closed, eastward window blind,
Something wells up in my heart,
Most of joy and hope a part.

Burns the morning's warming glow
Over wastes of ice and snow;
Over spaces chill and bare,
Life and love are in the air.
With the year that is to be
Throbs my heart in sympathy.
Springward turns the whole world's mind,
Sleep and death are left behind.

In the hot, glad afternoons,
When the whole world melts and swoons
In a garment of thin haze
Over woods and rude roadways,

And the landscape, chill and wan,
Softer aspect taketh on;
Then my steps to southward turn
Where the sloping sun doth burn.

Then my heart within me sings
Lyrics of the world's dead springs;
Something mystic, magical,
Hovers, glamours over all;
Even the osiers, red and yellow,
Prophesy each to its fellow;
Every voice and note I hear
Whispers of the pulsing year.

Cackling fowls in southward barns,
Wild notes over sheeted tarns,
Melted roadways, soiled snow,
Premature calling of a crow,

Fill my soul with reveries
As wells the upward sap in trees,
When my steps to southward turn
And the sloping sun doth burn.

Then at night, ere men have slept,
Across the stars a mist hath crept;
Then a film drapes the skies,
And the night hath softer eyes;
Something in the heaven aglow,
Something in the earth below,
Toward glad dreaming turns my brain,
And my heart grows young again.

LOVE.

Love came at dawn when all the world was fair,
When crimson glories, bloom, and song were rife;
Love came at dawn when hope's wings fanned the air,
And murmured, "I am life."

Love came at even when the day was done,
When heart and brain were tired, and slumber pressed;
Love came at eve, shut out the sinking sun,
And whispered, "I am rest."

A DECEMBER MORNING.

BREAKS in the wild and bleak December morn,
  Across shrunk woods and pallid skies like pearl:
  From hooded roofs white, sinuous smoke-wreaths curl
Into the clear, sharp air; great boughs, wind-torn
And storm-dismantled, sway from trunks forlorn.
  Under stark fences, snow-mists sift and swirl,
  And overhead, where night was wont to hurl
Her ghostly drift, white clouds, wind-steered, are borne.

By drifted ways I climb the eastern hills,
  And watch the wind-swayed maples creak and strain;
  The muffled beeches moan their wintry pain;
While over fields and frosty, silent rills,
The breaking day the great, grey silence fills
  With far-heard voice and stir of life again.

IN THE FREEDOM OF THE SPRING.

WHEN snows melt out and Winter breaks his chain,
And earth, released from her shrivelled woe,
Wakens beneath the warm suns come again,
And thawed streams widen in their overflow,
And woods with song and buddings gladder grow;
'Tis then I love to loose me from this life,
Its cares, its gridings, and its sordid strife,
And roam, kin-child with all earth's souls that glow.

Far out in great north woods, wind-rocked and swung,
When the soft south has warmed the wintry earth,
In those glad days when lusty life is young,
To bloom with waxen petals, spring's new birth,

And brawling brooklets haste in murmurous mirth;
  I slip life's leash with freedom of the spring,
  While the young year in its first love doth fling
New joys, new beauties, round the grey world's girth.

Here in hushed dells, by mossy crags and steeps,
  Where silent pools stand moorèd in the air,
Under the shade of woodlands, shy, cool deeps,
  Loved by lone creatures stealing to loiter there:
The timid fawn, the loping, shadowy hare,
  The wily lynx, who secret haunts his prey;
  Here flutter of wings, athwart the drowsèd day,
Wakes Solitude from out her hidden lair.

Big swollen rivers, haunting still, deep woods,
  Where dawn is midnight and faint dawn at noon,
Sing under shadows, pausing in shimmering moods
  Of inky silence, glimmering like the moon

In midnight's heaven; the while a drowsy tune
  The singing shallows make to shine and shade,
  While through the budding boughs the warm winds wade,
Sowing in petals white the year's first rune.

The low of kine comes in from farms afar,
  The chopper's axe rings blithely down the wind,
And here at even comes the first pale star,
  In the soft heaven over the woods behind
Where the warm south hath blown in, bland and kind;
  'Tis here I love to be; to feel my heart
  Wake with the season's in its first glad start,
When the young year gropes slow for heart and mind.

Far out in maple woods, with laugh and song,
  The jocund sugar-makers ease their toil
With mirth, the sunny, melting hours along,
  Where, brim with sap, the great iron kettles boil,

And troughs spill over with their amber spoil
  Of generous maples; evening skies loom soft
  With veil of stars, in heaven's deep wells aloft,
Where great mossed branches lift and spread and coil.

Out in far wastes and under sun-pierced glades,
  Where naked boughs put forth their misty buds,
The snows are rotting, and the thin ice fades
Like wasting steel; alone in gloom of woods,
The soilèd drifts still lift their shrunken hoods
  In storm-swathed hollows; by far river shores
  The sun-warmed wind hath eaten the ice in cores,
Winnowing with warmth the frosty solitudes.

The year hath draped his mantle of beauty on,
  And tuned his pipe to melody once more;
All weazened faces put new youth upon,
  And I am fain to learn the young year's lore;

His wisdom taught of heaven and wood and shore;
  To drink anew of life's fresh ecstasy,
  To dream new love in sky and field and tree,
Where Spring's first footsteps blossom the forest floor.

THE CHILDREN OF THE FOAM.

THE CHILDREN OF THE FOAM.

OUT forever and forever,
Where our tresses glint and shiver
  On the icy, moonlit air;
Come we from a land of gloaming,
Children lost, forever homing,
  Never, never reaching there;
Ride we, ride we, ever faster,
Driven by our demon master,
  The wild wind in his despair.
Ride we, ride we, ever home,
Wan, white children of the foam.

In the wild October dawning,
When the heaven's angry awning
  Leans to lakeward, bleak and drear;
And along the black, wet ledges,
Under icy, caverned edges,
  Breaks the lake in maddened fear;
And the woods in shore are moaning;
Then you hear our weird intoning,
  Mad, late children of the year;
Ride we, ride we, ever home,
Lost, white children of the foam.

All grey day, the black sky under,
Where the beaches moan and thunder,
  Where the breakers spume and comb;
You may hear our riding, riding,
You may hear our voices chiding,
  Under glimmer, under gloam;

Like a far-off infant wailing,
You may hear our hailing, hailing,
  For the voices of our home;
Ride we, ride we, ever home,
Haunted children of the foam.

And at midnight, when the glimmer
Of the moon grows dank and dimmer,
  Then we lift our gleaming eyes;
Then you see our white arms tossing,
Our wan breasts the moon embossing,
  Under gloom of lake and skies;
You may hear our mournful chanting,
And our voices haunting, haunting,
  Through the night's mad melodies:
Riding, riding, ever home,
Wild, white children of the foam.

There forever and forever,
Will no demon-hate dissever
  Peace and sleep and rest and dream;
There is neither fear nor fret there
When the tired children get there,
  Only dews and pallid beam
Fall in gentle peace and sadness
Over long surcease of madness,
  From hushed skies that gleam and gleam:
In the longed-for, sought-for home
Of the children of the foam.

There the streets are hushed and restful,
And of dreams is every breast full,
  With the sleep that tired eyes wear;
There the city hath long quiet
From the madness and the riot,
  From the failing hearts of care;

Balm of peacefulness ingliding,
Dream we through our riding, riding,
  As we homeward, homeward fare;
Riding, riding, ever home,
Wild, white children of the foam.

Under pallid moonlight beaming,
Under stars of midnight gleaming,
  And the ebon arch of night;
Round the rosy edge of morning,
You may hear our distant horning,
  You may mark our phantom flight;
Riding, riding, ever faster,
Driven by our demon master,
  Under darkness, under light;
Ride we, ride we, ever home,
Wild, white children of the foam.

HOW ONE WINTER CAME IN THE LAKE REGION.

FOR weeks and weeks the autumn world stood still,
  Clothed in the shadow of a smoky haze;
The fields were dead, the wind had lost its will,
And all the lands were hushed by wood and hill,
  In those grey, withered days.

Behind a mist the blear sun rose and set,
  At night the moon would nestle in a cloud;
The fisherman, a ghost, did cast his net;
The lake its shores forgot to chafe and fret,
  And hushed its caverns loud.

Far in the smoky woods the birds were mute,
  Save that from blackened tree a jay would scream,
Or far in swamps the lizard's lonesome lute
Would pipe in thirst, or by some gnarlèd root
  The tree-toad trilled his dream.

From day to day still hushed the season's mood,
  The streams stayed in their runnels shrunk and dry;
Suns rose aghast by wave and shore and wood,
And all the world, with ominous silence, stood
  In weird expectancy:

When one strange night the sun like blood went down,
  Flooding the heavens in a ruddy hue;
Red grew the lake, the sere fields parched and brown,
Red grew the marshes where the creeks stole down,
  But never a wind-breath blew.

That night I felt the winter in my veins,
  A joyous tremor of the icy glow;
And woke to hear the north's wild vibrant strains,
While far and wide, by withered woods and plains,
  Fast fell the driving snow.

MIDWINTER STORM IN THE LAKE REGION.

RISES the wild, red dawn over the icicled edges
Of black, wet, cavernous rocks, sheeted and winter-scarred,
And heaving of grey-green waves, foaming the ice-blocks and ledges,
Into this region of death, sky-bounded, solitude-barred.

Turned to the cold kiss of dawn, gilding their weird, dark faces,
Lift the cyclopean rocks, silent, motionless, bare;
Where high on each haggard front, in deep-plowed, passionate traces
The storm hath graven his madness, the night hath furrowed her care.

Out of the far, grey skies comes the dread north with
his blowing,
That chills the warm blood in the veins, and cuts to
the heart like fate.
Quick as the fall of a leaf the lake-world is white with
his snowing,
Quick as the flash of a blade the waters are black
with his hate.

God pity the sad-fated vessels that over these waters are
driven
To meet the rude shock of his strength and shudder
at blast of his breath;
God pity the tempest-drave sailors, for here naught on
wave or in heaven
Is heard but the hate of the night, the merciless grind-
ing of death.

TO THE LAKES.

WITH purple glow at even,
  With crimson waves at dawn,
Cool bending blue of heaven,
  O blue lakes pulsing on;
Lone haunts of wilding creatures dead to wrong;
  Your trance of mystic beauty
  Is wove into my song.

I know no gladder dreaming
  In all the haunts of men,
I know no silent seeming
  Like to your shore and fen;

No world of restful beauty like your world
Of curvèd shores and waters,
In sunlight vapors furled.

I pass and repass under
Your depths of peaceful blue,
You dream your wild, hushed wonder
Mine aching heart into;
And all the care and unrest pass away
Like night's grey, haunted shadows
At the red birth of day.

You lie in moon-white splendour
Beneath the northern sky,
Your voices soft and tender
In dream-worlds fade and die,
In whispering beaches, haunted bays and capes,
Where mists of dawn and midnight
Drift past in spectral shapes.

Beside your far north beaches,
Comes late the quickening spring;
With soft, voluptuous speeches
The summer, lingering,
Fans with hot winds your breasts so still and wide,
Where June, with trancèd silence,
Drifts over shore and tide.

Beneath great crags the larches,
By some lone, northern bay,
Bend, as the strong wind marches
Out of the dull, north day,
Horning along the borders of the night,
With icèd, chopping waters
Out in the shivering light.

Here the white winter's fingers
Tip with dull fires the dawn,
Where the pale morning lingers
By stretches bleak and wan;

Kindling the icèd capes with heatless glow,
That renders cold and colder
Lone waters, rocks and snow.

Here in the glad September,
When all the woods are red
And gold, and hearts remember
The long days that are dead;
And all the world is mantled in a haze;
And the wind, a mad musician,
Melodious makes the days;

And the nights are still, and slumber
Holds all the frosty ground,
And the white stars whose number
In God's great books are found,
Gird with pale flames the spangled, frosty sky;
By white, moon-curvèd beaches
The haunted hours go by.

MOONLIGHT.

THE moonlight on this beach lies pallidly,
  And on the waters in a white track dreams,
  Where ripples pulsate under misty beams.
Far out the night lifts vast and shadowy,
Fear-haunted, where the dim, white headlands lie,
  And chants the lake the dark's wild frighted themes
  In far-heard thunders. Here the silence teems
With frensy's sweet and frosted phantasy.

This is the realm of lovers, and across
  This silvery web two shadows come and go.
  Outside the world sleeps with its freight of woe,
Its human load of haggard pain and loss;
  But these two dream, where elfin torches glow
And wind-stirred boughs their snowy foliage toss.

ON A SUMMER SHORE.

LONG years have gone, and yet it seems
  But scarce an hour ago,
I lay upon a moss-grown rock,
  And watched the ebb and flow
Of waters, where cool shades above
  Glassed in cool depths below.

You stood beside me sweet and fair,
  A basket on your arm,
Red-heaped with luscious fruit we'd picked
  Down at the old shore farm;
You stood and in the shore-wood made
  A picture glad and warm.

Like heaving pearl the blue bay rocked
  Against its limestone wall,
Far off in reeling dreams of blue
  The heavens seemed to fall
About the world, and there you stood,
  Unconscious, queen of all.

From far-off fields the low of kine,
  Soft bird-notes, airy streams,
That stole in here,' far, broken notes
  Of all the day's hushed dreams;
And you, one slender shaft of light,
  In all the world's wide gleams.

We spoke no love, for I was shy,
  And you were shyer then;
Mine was a boy's faint heart, and yours
  Still outside of love's ken;

But such sweet moments are full rare
  In barren years of men.

And often when the heart is worn
  And life grows sorrow-wise,
I dream again a blue, north bay,
  A gleam of summer skies;
And by my side a young girl stands
  With heaven in her eyes.

You are a dream, a face, a wraith,
  You drift across my pain,
I lock you in my sacred past
  Where all love's ghosts remain;
But life hath nought for me so sweet
  As you can bring again.

ON THE SHORE.

AGE.

WITH golden spicèd dreams blows in the dawn,
  About the cool blue bosom of the lake;
  Far over wave and shore wild voices wake,
The watery curves and windy reeds upon,
Where the young glory of the day dreams on;
  And wingèd creatures haunts of sleep forsake,
  And dreams and silence their dim ways betake
Round the grey edge where lidded night hath gone.

Here all is young and glad, the laughing shore
  The sunshine, the glad birds, no memories
  On haggard faces wistful to forget;
Save yon old man beside the rude hut door,
With palsied hands, chin bending to his knees,
  Mending dead youth in meshes of a net.

BROWNING.

TO MIGHTY DEATH CONCERNING ROBERT BROWNING.

GREAT Warder of those mists forever yawning,
  And whence no soul returns that wanders through
Into some muffled midnight or white dawning,
  Into strange peace no love hath proven true;
  Whom we know now no more than Homer knew,
Or Plato's master ere the hemlock drink
Charmed his great soul across thy shadowed brink.

O mighty Death, teach us of our great brother,
  Whose sight was deep and spirit strong like wine;
Long will it be before earth knows another
  Like unto him who worked the heart's deep mine,

And chiselled from the chaos sparks divine:
Who delved so long beneath, he failed to care
How formed his crystal heaps in outer air.

Lord of all song but for the lack of caring,
When high in lyric flight his heart did lift,
No lesser brother pinioned where its faring
Seemed reaching up to God through skyey rift;
What demon chained his mighty soul to drift
In mystic visions, meaningless and long,
Who might have piped the world's youth back in song?

'Twixt him and us deep silences are falling,
For his is rest and ours awhile to moan;
We call through dark and still we keep on calling,
And grope about our prison-hearts of stone;
And hear no voice but echo of our own;
We on, he back, beneath the spangled dark,
Like outbound bark that vanisheth from bark.

Where hath he fared, and what glad mystic vision
  Hath wrapt his soul? What mighty peace of night?
What good knows he? What sweet, long-lost elysian
  Doth he reclaim? What reveries of delight?
  In what far borders wings his strenuous flight?
This lore-wrapt seer, song's mightiest, I trow,
Who knew so much, what wisdom hath he now?

O great, kind Death, whom men call falsely cruel,
  Read us the riddle, life's best, latest friend;
In what weird matrix formeth love's bright jewel?
  In our beginning do we know our end?
  Hath he gone back with some old past to blend?
Or doth he on to other regions fare,
Recrystallized in some diviner air?

Can he take up the songs he failed in singing?
  Can he make clear what here seemed meaningless?

Can his soul soar, nor ever tire of winging?
  Or doth he feel our earth-born giddiness?
  For all old wounds hath he now love's redress?
Or lost in dreamings, by thy weird love kissed,
Is his great soul still rounded by a mist?

There is a land where summer, spring, nor winter,
  Nor noon, nor night, nor morning's holy prime,
Nor love, nor hate, nor hope can ever enter,
  A dreamless land, beyond the date of time;
  A land of eld and age and hoary rime,
Of sleep's long frosts, where sword and armour rust,
And shackles fall from hands that turn to dust.

Here all may sleep, for no dread warder's warning
  Can come with clang of care and garish day;
They sleep the sleep of night that knows no morning,
  No fierce noon-heats or chill at evening grey;
  No sound of those who watch or weep or pray

May enter here to stir the long, long rest
Of those who slumber on oblivion's breast.

Long weaned of life's mad throe and time's weird glory,
  Stilled hands on breast, sleep closely side by side,
The hearts that read and those who told earth's story,
  The necks that bent, the brows that rose in pride:
  But one event for all who here abide,
The wise, the fool, the despot and the slave,
One common dust in one great common grave.

* * * * *

And he who met so calm thy salutation,
  When thou didst hail him softly, "Peace, be still!"
Forsaking men and toil and adulation,
  Smoothed his great brow and bowed him to thy will;
  And went with thee meet lordly place to fill,
In the great minster walls where love doth keep
The genius of a nation in its sleep.

* * * * *

Forgive these winter songs, O great Life-Master,
  These halting rhymes, O strong and puissant Death:
Our sight is small, but thine is vast and vaster;
  Thy knowledge lives, ours dwindles with a breath.
  Forgive these rhymes on him who slumbereth;
Who was too great for mine unworthy pen
To do him grace, King Singer of singing men.

THE DEAD LEADER.

JUNE 10, 1891.

LET the sad drums mutter low,
And the serried ranks move slow,
And the thousand hearts beat hushed along the street;
For a mighty heart is still,
And a great, unconquered will,
Hath passed to meet the conqueror all must meet.

Outworn without assoil
From a great life's lengthened toil,
Laurelled with a half a century's fame;

From the care and adulation
To the heart-throb of the nation
He hath passed to be a memory and a name.

With banners draped and furled,
'Mid the sorrow of a world,
We lay him down with fitting pomp and state,
With slumber in his breast,
To his long, eternal rest
We lay him down, this man who made us great.

Him of the wider vision,
Who had one hope, elysian,
To mould a mighty empire toward the west;
Who through the hostile years,
'Mid the wrangling words, like spears,
Still bore this titan vision in his breast.

God gave this highest honour
To the nation, that upon her
He was spared to lay the magic of his hand;
Then to live to see the greatness
Of his noble works, completeness,
Then to pass to rest belovèd by his land.

We stand at death's dim gates
Where his mighty soul awaits
Somewhere the long, long silence of the years.
And the marble of his lips
Doth all our woe eclipse,
Death's awful peace rolls back upon our tears.

Greater than all sorrow
That our hearts can borrow;
Loftier than our fleeting, human praise,

He hath calmness, great and grim,
That death hath granted him,
The wisest and the mightiest of our days.

Let the sad drums mutter low,
And the serried ranks move slow,
And the thousand hearts beat hushed along the street;
For a mighty heart is still,
And a great, unconquered will,
Hath passed to meet the conqueror all must meet.

www.ingramcontent.com/pod-product-compliance
Lightning Source LLC
Chambersburg PA
CBHW031440160426
43195CB00010BB/804
9783744714037